ONCE UPON A TIME ...IN EGYPT

Samir M. Zoghby

Bethesda Communications Group

Copyright © Samir M. Zoghby 2018

Published by the Bethesda Communications Group
4816 Montgomery Lane
Bethesda, MD 20814
www.bcgpub.com

ISBN-13: 978-1-7321501-3-3
ISBN-10: 1-7321501-3-3

All drawings are by Samir M. Zoghby.

To my children, Natasha and Michel

With all my love, Dad

Contents

Preface 7
Introduction 11
Simplified phonology 13
1. Nocturnal Meetings of the Initiates 14
2. Lunch Time and Intrusive Tourism 16
3. Siblings and Sweet Potatoes 20
4. Dust to Dust. R.I.P. 22
5. Mama 'Aishah at the Pita Bread Oven 24
6. Don't Frown at Me…I'm Following! 26
7. Careless Lady in a Carriage in Old Cairo 28
8. The Saga of the *Bani Hilal* *30*
9. The Old Man's Cane Echoed in the Covered Market ... 34
10. Competition is Tough 36
11. Grandpa Needs a Rest… 38
12. Tirmis Tangy and Salty 40
13. Don't Tell Me How To Carve the Meat! 42
14. The Sweet Smell of Ismaïlia Melons 44
15. The Young Qena Diogenes 46
16. Gossiping Al Fresco 48
17. And Then, I Told Him… 52
18. Old Man and His Donkey 54
19. The Ornithologist in His Milieu 56
20. The Village Shisha Is Still the Best! 58
21. Morning Trades 60
22. Camel Transaction 62
23. Village Cunning 66
24. The Redskins in Aswan 68
25. Lost in His Newspaper 70
26. Ford and Chevrolet Trucks on Dusty Roads 74
27. The Legacy of Hassan al-Banna 76
28. Pink Nightgown and Somber Darks 80
29. Hurry Up…We Must Catch the Train 82
30. Free Parking 84
31. Jerusalem Blue Glass Artist 86
32. Noon Prayer 88
33. You Squeeze Them, You Buy Them! 90

34. Working Alabaster in 113 F. Temperature 92
35. The Welcome and the Threat 94
36. Dervishes for Tourists 96
37. Conviviality Among Drying Sheets 100
38. To Hit or Not To Hit? 102
39. The New Generation Doesn't Known How... 104
40. Darting Looks and Plumpness 106
41. Enough is Enough! 110
42. The Meal the Pharaohs Ate 112
43. Life is Suffering 116
44. Veterans of the Dark Days 118
45. The Chanting of the Word of God 122

Preface

" One is not from a country, one is from one's childhood"
                                                    Saint-Exupéry

Joseph Tubiana and I met Samir Zoghby in Chad in 1991, during an International Colloquium on *Chadian Identity*.
   Samir, who at the time was Division Chief at the United States Agency for International Development (USAID), participated in this colloquium and rapidly established a rapport with some of the participants coming from various countries by inviting those he wanted to know better. Our friendship goes back to that time about twenty-five years ago. It was then a succession of meetings in Paris, N'Djamena, and also Washington.
   In N'Djamena we were staying at his house, where he had set up a special place for us with welcome notes pinned on doors and walls; he also had set up an area covered with sumptuous rugs where we were able to receive in a convivial manner our informants to carry out our research and future enquiries.
   But who was Samir, this short man, rotund, jovial and smiling? A polyglot handling, Arabic, French, English and many other languages. A man of immense culture, curious about others, and an amateur of art and culture.
   He was born in Egypt and lived there his first twenty years. Born of a Syro-Lebanese father and a Czech mother, he was a student at the French school of the Suez Canal Company in Ismaïlia, where his father worked, but also a student at the Arabic-speaking Greek Catholic school in Cairo, living in an international environment where all the nationalities were represented as well as all the social strata and religions. What a chance to be immersed in all these potentials, to receive these different riches. Yet, one had to know how to grab the opportunities and turn them to good account. It was, it seems to me, Samir's destiny.
   Has drawing always been for him a privileged means of expression? I could not tell, but since I have known him, I always

saw him with a small notebook on which he rapidly drew drawings with felt-tip pen where appeared birds, reptiles, peasants, and multiple abstract designs...during the long and tedious phone conversations where dream allowed him to assume the platitude of the exchange with his interlocutor without getting irritated while remaining attentive to his request; only the tracing hand allowed the evasion. We were fascinated by his large chimeric birds with sparkling colors, one of which became the logo of the "Pour Mieux Connaître le Tchad" collection.

Today, Samir gives us a series of felt pen drawings bringing to life the Egyptian society of his youth. He left Egypt sixty years ago, became an American, and has lived with curiosity and passion in a number of African countries: Tunisia, Upper Volta, Morocco, Chad, Namibia and Yemen; but Egypt, although he never went back, never left him.

It is the Egypt of his youth that we meet again in these drawings done sixty years later in Washington: memories, descriptions, and historical research merge to give us a chance to see this teeming life that made us feel like quoting this sentence remembered from a reading: *"One is not from a country, one is from one's childhood."* Thank you, Samir, for making us discover all these small crafts that have sometimes disappeared, what we can discern in the doors ajar. Thank you for this life sketched with the precision of a photographer and with an undertone of humor always present: the young man who is late and we see his nose showing at the edge of the page, the cat roaming in the shop waiting for a good morsel, the adventurous small mouse, the perfidious snake sliding in the midst of people, the stray dog, the reddish glow of the brasero, the fuming incense, and the quavering light of candles. One can hear the sounds, hear the rhythm of the drums, and one smells the aroma of Egyptian dishes and sees the cart with its oven on which sweet potatoes are roasting, bringing us gourmand fragrances. Our curiosity will be satisfied in the minute descriptions of clothes in cotton and silk where shimmering beautiful colors appear like an evidence in these drawings, mind you in black and white, in the embroidered caps and the turbans in delicate cotton fabric, as well as the luxuriance of beards, some bushy, others pointed, and expressive mustaches, some arrogant, some modest, and others conquering. The "bearded ones," members of the Muslim Brothers Association, created in 1928, appear already in Egyptian daily life.

One will also find in these drawings the ushering in of modernism with the tourists, attracted by the publicity, but not always respectful of national customs, the presence of terrorists, the trivialization of modern weapons, such as the Kalashnikov, and the scourge of plastic bags embedded in the ground and clinging to the trees. Sad reality is described, but also nostalgia of yesteryears

The traditional bouts with sticks rub shoulders with the marble cutter wearing a denim outfit, a cigarette hanging from his lips, laboring behind modern machines. The large Cairo railways station offers us an interesting historical perspective with the alternation of art works according to what the times wants to symbolize.

There is no specific order in the presentation of the various drawings. One could easily reshuffle them like a deck of cards and invert them: they appear one after the other randomly following the wandering in the streets. Each drawing is constructed around some characters, but from the ensemble rises an exuberance that represents—indeed, for he who has spent even a brief time in Cairo—the soul of the city. Cars go side by side with horse or donkey-drawn carts as well as the small herds of sheep or the camel sold by its owner in the market; the fishmonger is next to the merchant of oil or perfumes, and the modest peddlers selling bread, fava, licorice, and tamarind-flavored drinks thread their way in the midst of the strollers. Life is omnipresent.

One will plunge into these drawings and be carried away by their magic or take time to decode them with the help of the precise and amused comments offered by the author.

It is illusory to want to classify these drawings under any label, and yet a notation by Elie Faure, taken from his chapter on Egypt, seems to me to offer Samir's drawings a poetical categorization of great accuracy:

The Egyptian drawing is a writing that must be learned. But when you know it well...[all the characters] live ingeniously, and their silence is populated with animation and whispers!"
Histoire de l'Art, 1909, réédition Bartillat, 2010, Livre V: 100 -101).

Marie-José Tubiana
Honorary Research Director at the CNRS
25 April 2016

Introduction

Kan yama kaan fi qadiim al-zamaan, "Once upon a time, O how many times/ a long time ago." Thus began all grandmothers' stories in Egypt—this Egypt that I left in 1953 for the American University of Beirut in Lebanon, and then left in 1957 for the United States, never to return to live there.

I was born in Egypt of a Syro-Lebanese father and a Czech mother. I lived in Ismaïlia, a city dominated and controlled during my youth by the French Suez Canal Company and the British army. I was circumcised by Hakham Israel. After the intervention he told my parents in jest, "He is one of us. I called him Samuel."

From my birth in 1932 until my departure in 1953, I lived a quasi-schizophrenic existence at two levels. At one level, it was a life divided between my European family, the Altenburgers, and my Cairene family, the Zoghbys; between the kissing of ladies' hands, which was still required by European etiquette, and the streets swarming with people from the Faggalah and Daher Quarters in Cairo with its cacophony and commotion where people talked loud and hard; between the black earth of the Nile River banks and the yellow sand of the Suez Canal; between the French school of the Suez Canal Company run by Bretons brothers from Ploërmel in Brittany and the Arabic-speaking high school of our Greek-Catholic community of Cairo; between French, Dutch, White Russian, Italian, Yugoslav, Greek, Maltese, and English friends in Ismaïlia and the sons of Muslim big land-owners, Coptic doctors, Syro-Lebanese business tycoons, Sephardic Jews, and Saudi nouveaux riches who were my comrades at the Cairo High School. It was as different as day and night. At another level of dichotomy was the ambiguous position of the majority of the Syro-Lebanese community, who felt that they were from Egypt but never felt Egyptian. We were the *Khawagaat*[1] (singular *Khawaagah*), the "Misters." This naming has gone through a great mutation. During the 20s and 30s, it was a sign of respect—I would say almost admiration—that became with time an insult

---

[1] "Indeed, Christians of Syrian origin constituted part of the foreign (European) community in Egypt." Hisham Sharabi, *Arab Intellectuals and the West: the Formative Years*, Baltimore, The Johns Hopkins University Press, 1970, p. 20.

and a call of disdain.

And yet, I left Egypt but Egypt never left me. Yes, Egypt was me, but was it truly me? It would need years on the sofa of the ethnopsychiatrist Tobie Nathan, who was born in Egypt, to understand!

Egypt had remained in me as a refuge during my hard years in Washington. My Egypt was my carefree life in Ismaïlia, it was the Greek-Catholic Cathedral of Faggalah, it was the belly dancer Tahia Carioca—people said she was from Ismaïlia—and the belly dancer Samia Gamal, it was the Nagib al-Rihani Theater and the play "Hassan, Morkos we Cohen," a parody full of humor and love of the three religions and their co-religionists.

I was homesick. I felt nostalgia not for a place in space, but for a slice of history in a time that was no more. A Bani Zoghba once again a nomad!

These drawings done in Washington represent childhood memories that have not left me after more than 85 years, but it was also thanks to the Internet that I was able to bring to the surface of memory many images and recollections from Egypt, images I had thought gone forever. The stories are a combination of descriptions of the drawings, historical events linked to them, and personal memories. It is also a history of my Egypt that is obviously not today's Egypt, which I barely recognize. However, the *noktah,* or joke (often political), has remained a link between the various Egypts throughout history. Such a *noktah* is vibrant, alive, and insolent despite the political storms.

To further add to the skein of my emotional threads, one must include 60 years in the United States, coming to know and love my new home and serving the federal government for more than 30 years. I now reside in Iva, South Carolina.

Today at 86, memories are becoming blurred, and I have the impression that I am a dinosaur going with nostalgia through pages of drawings of the good old days.

I have also included sayings and vignettes culled from the distant past.

Samir M. Zoghby

Simplified phonology

Consonnants

/h/ - Voiceless pharyngeal fricative - No equivalent in English. Sounds like in ha-ha, air is expelled from the belly with force.
/kh/ - Voiceless velar fricative - like in wehrmacht in German and mujer in Spanish.
/gh/ - Voiced uvular fricative - like the parisian /r/ and grama in Greek.
/h\/ - Voiceless Glottal fricative - like a very British "home".
/?/ - Glottal stop - produced by obstructing airflow in the glottis. The glottal stop is not used in initial position.
/'/ Voiced pharyngeal fricative - a creaky-voiced epiglottal consonant articulated in the pharynx
The /h/ in final position represent the /t/ marbutah.
The difference between pharyngealized and non-pharyngealized is not indicated
Stress is represented by a double consonant .

Vowels

Length is represented by a doubled vowel as in kifaayah (enough).

Samir M. Zoghby

1. Nocturnal Meetings of the Initiates

Disciples surround a teacher during a nocturnal session of spiritual communion in the wavering light of candles and the comforting heat of a brazier. This drawing is a pure product of my imagination. However, It reminds me of the ceremonies of *zaar* (possession ceremony)[1] that I witnessed through the half-open doors from which emanated a thick wisp of incense as I walked through the working class neighborhood of Qubaisi in Cairo. One could hear the halting rhythm of multiple *Allah Hayy* (God is Alive), chanted by hoarse voices accompanied by the beatings of *tablah*, (drum), in a dizzying and frenzied crescendo.

The proverbial late-comer is there; he had risked finding himself out of the drawing. The disciples wear the traditional *galabiyyah* (ample long garment, in cotton for the modest peasant and often in silk for the notables.)They are all wearing a *ta?iyyah* (a skullcap woven with bright colors with traditional geometric designs). Most of the disciples wear a mustache.

The master has a beard and a *'immah* (turban), that indicates his rank and status.

---

1 Zaar is a possession ceremony, but more specifically of adorcism where bewitched women accept the possessive genie and do not try to exorcise and expel it. The sessions consist of dances at a frenzied rhythm with a frenetic music guided by the *Kudiya*, the holder of the genies' secrets. Women dance whirling and chanting *Allah Hayy* (God is alive), going faster and faster until they reach a state of trance and physical exhaustion.

Once Upon a Time...in Egypt

2. Lunch Time and Intrusive Tourism

This composition is inspired by the situation of international tourism in the touristic regions of Egypt in general and Karnak and Luxor (Upper Egypt) in particular.

The Muslim fundamentalists exploit this soft underbelly of Egypt by attacking tourists and threatening an essential industry of the country. In 2010, 14.7 million tourists visited Egypt with a revenue of 12.5 billion dollars for the state. In 2015, the statistics show an increase in the flux of tourists by 10 to 15% that dropped dramatically after the downing of the Russian Metrojet plane in October 2015.

The Egyptian Government has, by necessity, deployed a whole security structure to protect the tourist sites often with a measure of success. Nevertheless, it could not prevent certain disasters such as the massacre in Luxor of 62 tourists, on November 17, 1997, and the attack of a bus at the Saint Catherine monastery in the Sinai, on October 16, 2014 that killed two South Korean tourists and an Egyptian driver. *Ansaar Beit al-Maqdis,*[2] a terrorist group that claimed the responsibility for the attack, had posted a warning to the tourists on its Twitter account. The attack on October 31st 2015 against flight 9268 of the Russian Company Metrojet leaving Sharm el-Sheikh was a terrible blow to tourism in Egypt. There were 224 victims and once again *Ansaar Beit al-*

---

2 Ansaar Beit al-Maqdis (The Defenders of Jerusalem) a terrorist group that operates in the Sinai. They mainly attack Egyptian military forces and have joined DAESH since 2014.

Once Upon a Time...in Egypt

Samir M. Zoghby

Maqdis claimed responsibility for the attack.

Officers, soldiers and agents in mufti take a quick meal before rejoining their posts. There is the officer with a walkie-talkie; a soldier carrying the ever-present Kalashnikov, and the agent in mufti, with his big mustache, also carrying a Kalashnikov. The latter is also wearing an *'immah* (turban) covering a skullcap with geometric designs and an ample cashmere scarf, imported from India, probably via Yemen.

The policemen are settled around a *tabliyyah* (a low and round wooden table) covered with many dishes in enamelware full of *falaafel* (fried balls made of chickpeas), *bamiah* (okra) cooked in a tomato sauce, *koftah* (meat balls); without forgetting the *fuul medammis* (simmered fava) flavored with olive oil and lemon which is the Egyptian national dish without class distinction; raw cucumbers and green onions; all served with round Arabic bread (*'eish baladi*).

A tourist and her children have discovered the discreet spot of the policemen. She takes pictures of this private moment maybe without asking permission to do so...but who knows?...

A viper speeds towards the unaware sparrow. The tourist has not noticed the snake either.

Harvard Business School and a missed opportunity

One day at AUB, I was sitting alone in the cafeteria when a tall American came by with his tray and asked if he could sit at my table. I agreed and we talked about school, how well I was doing, and when I was finishing school. He started talking about the Harvard Business School and the scholarships they had. He then asked if I were interested in applying for a scholarship. To this day, I am still kicking myself for telling him that I was not interested in business. He nodded, saying fine. He later told me that he was the dean of the Harvard Business School and was on a recruiting trip!

Cupid and the classroom

At the University of Beirut, competition was ferocious to date the few American girls who studied there. In Chemistry 101, I had as my teacher a young American preparing for her MS in that field. I started by teaching her French, then later on, many other things. I hated chemistry, but I was counting on Jo, my teacher. The day of the exam, she flunked me! Back home, I expressed my surprise. Her answer: A relationship is a relationship and the classroom is the classroom. A word to the wise!

3. Siblings and Sweet Potatoes

An old man sitting on a *dekkah* (a wooden bench decorated with geometric designs carved in the wood), looks as the world pass by. The bench is covered with braided straw.

The old man wears a greying beard and a turban, as well as a light scarf. His cane helps him walk, but it is also a symbol of authority that demands respect and consideration. He is surrounded by his sons. The eldest is sitting by his father and shares a glass of tea. The others are respectfully standing behind their father. The two glasses of strong and scalding tea are set on a small three-legged brass table.

In the back, above a low wall, a *musharrabiyyah* (wooden latticed screen formed by the patient and skillful assembly of lathe-worked multiple pieces of wood). The screen often separates and protects the wives' quarters.

An itinerant seller pushes his cart loaded with sweet potatoes much appreciated by the passersby. The cart is also decorated with geometrical forms carved into the wood and often painted in bright colors. The oven tied to the cart is forged by skilled blacksmiths.

Once Upon a Time...in Egypt

Samir M. Zoghby

4. Dust to Dust. R.I.P.

Wake where friends of the deceased share a moment of meditation and prayers. The body is unusually wrapped in strips of cotton that replace the more usual *kafan* (shroud) traditionally cut in one single piece of white cotton cloth in which the body is wrapped. A brazier gives off a wisp of incense.

All wear a *galabiyyah* (long cotton garment). Some wear a *sedeeri* (vest) under the *galabiyyah*. This latter is often made of silk with shimmering colors with a row of buttons. Most of the persons sport a *ta?iyyah* (skullcap), and another wears a turban. A youngster has a conic fez that is out of fashion since the Nasser revolution of 1952. It was the symbol of the bourgeois *effendi* before the revolution.

Once Upon a Time...in Egypt

Samir M. Zoghby

5. Mama 'Aishah at the Pita Bread Oven

A traditional bakery. The woman sitting in front of the open oven is putting in the kiln a *baladi* round popular bread. She has her head covered with a colorful scarf and has rolled up her sleeves: given her age, she can allow herself to do so. Her colleague behind the counter is more discreetly dressed and her head is covered with a veil.

The two clients are modestly dressed, one with a scarf around her head, and the other with a simple veil. On the other hand the dresses are long and go all the way to the ground. The two children look with envy at the European *baguettes* as well as the tarts and the *baladi* bread pulled out of the wood oven. The counter is covered with ceramic tiles.

Once Upon a Time...in Egypt

6. Don't Frown at Me...I'm Following!

Abu-Gamaal al-'attaar (the father of Gamaal the perfumer), as the sign indicates, sells perfumes and aromas. He also sells seasonal fruits. He wears a *galabiyyah* and a vest.

The clients represent a broad range of characters. The traditional housewife follows her husband at a respectable distance and carries her son on her shoulder. She is demurely dressed. The glance of the husband denotes a stern authoritarian. He wears a *kufiyyah* (red or black checkered scarf) that has become, since it was adopted by Yasser Arafat (to cover his baldness?), the symbol of anti-Zionist Palestinian resistance, and a coat to protect him from the cold. The old lady, talking to her grand-daughter dressed Western style, wears a veil over a modern blouse and skirt. The conservative young lady has loose garments that hide her forms and she has knotted a scarf around her head in the fashion of the day.

The wandering dog belongs to nobody and is interested in the kid who is precariously riding his bike. The decoration on the wall in the background denotes an old Cairo neighborhood with its probably ancient Ottoman and Mameluk residences.

Once Upon a Time...in Egypt

Samir M. Zoghby

7. Careless Lady in a Carriage in Old Cairo

The coachman of the *hantur* (horse-drawn carriage) takes a tourist for a visit to the old neighborhoods of Cairo. Her shorts, rather tight, shape her forms, which could attract rather unpleasant attention. She is very reckless!

The front of the house is decorated with a *musharabiyyah* (carved wooden lattice) behind which a well-covered woman observes the passage of the carriage. She looks at the passenger lightly dressed even for the torrid heat of Cairo during the summer. She does not miss the lecherous look of the coachman.

There is also the fruit seller dozing, probably overtaken by the heat. He watches with a sleepy eye his goods and an antiquated scale. The young student reading his book has given his shoes to the *bohyagi* (itinerant shoe-shine man) sitting by his kit. He is unaware, or unconcerned, about the sneering of the shoe-shine man who just became aware of the hole in the student's sock. He wears a vest under his *galabiyyah* as well as a fancy turban covering his *ta?iyyah* (skullcap).

Once Upon a Time...in Egypt

8. The Saga of the *Bani Hilal*

A Bedouin camp in the Egyptian desert. A musician, a kind of troubadour, plays on his *rabaabah* (two-cord string instrument), and generally singing ballads related to the history of the tribe. One of the best known ballads in the region is the *Taghribat Bani Hilal*.[3] It is a saga on the migration of the Bani Hilal tribe in the

---

3 *Taghribat Bani Hilal* is an epic poem relating the trials and tribulations of the Bani Hilal tribe and its allies during their voyage from Najd in the Arabian Peninsula to North Africa which they conquered in the 11th century. The origins of the saga is the revolt of the Zirid princes of Tunisia against the Fatimid Empire of Cairo. To get rid of turbulent tribes in Egypt and to punish the Zirids, the Fatimids "gave" this region to the Bani Hilal which they invaded like a flight of locusts. This put down the basis for the Arabization and Islamization of the region. Abu Zeid al-Hilaali became the fierce enemy of al-Zinaati Khalifah of the Zenata Berber tribe. The Taghribah is basically the story of this struggle. The saga is still sung in the working class neighborhood of cities and in the Egyptian countryside. But the repositories of the oral tradition are fast dying out.

My paternal uncle Archbishop Elias Zoghby had sent me, years ago, a painting on glass representing our ancestor al-Zoghby Diyaab Ibn Ghaanem busting, with his spear, the eye of Abu Sa'dah al-Zinaati Khalifah, the great enemy of the Bani Hilaal

Al-Zoghby Diyaab Ibn Ghaanem———Abu Sa'dah al-Zinaati Khalifah

Once Upon a Time...in Egypt

11th century, with the Bani Ka'b and Bani Zoghba among other tribes, and the conquest of North Africa. Ibn Khaldun, the Tunisian historian born in 1332 in an Andalusian family, relates in his *Prolegomena* that before the Hilalian invasion it was possible to walk in the shade of trees from Alexandria to Tangiers. After our passage, there was not a blade of grass, so they say!

During my work with USAID in Morocco in 1985, I was surprised to learn that my family name—Zoghby—was used in the Moroccan dialect as a synonym for "jinxed" and "trouble maker." When I asked my Moroccan friends for the reason of such labelling they answered with a smirk "Go and see how your ancestors have plundered the country in the 11th century." And since then the Zoghby and Ko'bi have been anathema in Morocco.

In front of the troubadour is a young man preparing coffee on a bed of live coals. He is holding a brass coffee pot. His neighbor, the chief of the clan, also wears a *galabiyyah*, but his head is covered by a *kufiyyah* held by a *'igaal* (a black rope braided out of camel hair). He also wears a heavy scarf made out of camel hair and savoring a very hot coffee in small cups making sure that his watch, symbol of his status, is well in evidence in front of the artist!

A woman wearing typically Bedouin jewelry is sitting at a distance with her child. In the background, a camel handler is crouching by his camel tethered to prevent it from escaping during the night. He is wearing a *kufiyyah* as a turban. The children are freely wandering in the encampment.

Thrift shop on wheels
Roba bekyah

When I was a kid, I used to see passing by in the streets of Ismaïlia an old man pushing an old cart. It was piled up with a variety of clothes. I could still hear him shout loud and clear, "Roba Bekya." It took me some time to understand that he meant "roba vecchia" which means old clothes in Italian.

Red watermelon
Hamaar we halaawah...

"By the knife...we'll open it and have you test and taste the redness and sweetness of the watermelon," used to boast the watermelon seller pushing his cart and goods.

9. The Old Man's Cane Echoed in the Covered Market

Steps are reverberating in the alleys of this old souk. The arches of the walls indicate an old covered neighborhood, lost in the mazes of the narrow streets of the old city.

The merchant, of a certain age, has a bushy beard and a turban. His stall is well stocked with heavy rolls of fabrics and children's clothes. Two women, one carrying her son, has covered her head with a veil well tucked around her neck. Her daughter, who is already wearing a veil, feels uneasy about the presence of the cat. The other woman is covered by an ample shawl. The two men carry rich scarves, one in cashmere on the shoulders of the beardless youth ; the other wrapped around the neck of the old one with a turban, greying beard, a cane and an imposing potbelly.

Once Upon a Time...in Egypt

10. Competition is Tough

A donkey saunters blithely. Its hoofs resonate on the pavement. An itinerant vendor carries a glass case on his head with prepared meals. The trestle on his shoulder will help him set down his heavy load to serve clients. Another vendor carries a large brass recipient on his shoulder that contains licorice, tamarin or lemon juices and ice. He has around his midriff a large belt with glasses that he will wash, after serving his clients, with water from the teapot suspended to his belt.

The satisfied smirk of his competitor is evident in spite of the contrived smile of the young man. The bearded one in *galabiyyah* and vest has a considerable advantage. He is pushing his heavy well-decorated cart loaded with three varieties of juices in large glass jars. He has a satisfied grin and stares at the poor sod crushed by the weight of his recipient. The youngster, who wears a *galabiyyah*, looks with envy at the fancy cart where glasses are clattering and clanking.

Once Upon a Time...in Egypt

11. Grandpa Needs a Rest...

In the back, stands a *sabiil* (a public fountain, gift of a rich and pious man to quench the thirst of passersby). It is the same principle as the Wallace drinking fountains in Paris. This fountain could well date from the medieval period.

Next to the fountain, the chicken vendor has installed his hen house. The sign reads *Dagaag al-Fayuum* (Fayum Chicken), a region of Upper Egypt well known for its poultry. He is patiently waiting for his clients. He is wearing a *galabiyyah*, a turban and a large scarf to protect him from the Cairo morning cold in winter.

Sitting in a row, an obese grandfather and his myopic wife rest on a stone slab with their grandchildren. The grandfather wears an ample *galabiyyah*, a skullcap and leans on a solid cane. His swollen feet are slid into sandals. His wife wears a veil on the head. She is overloaded with a length of fabric she just bought from the vendor in Chapter 9. The little girl does not have a veil and her dress comes probably from the same vendor. Her brother wears the traditional cotton *galabiyyah*. Behind them two women are fully wrapped up in their heavy veils. The vendor of *simiit* (sesame fritters), keeps an eye on his trestle and is preparing to serve the young man who is handing him a coin. He is dressed in European garbs and has a white woolen *ta?iyyah*.

Once Upon a Time...in Egypt

12. Tirmis Tangy and Salty

A farmer leads his sheep to market. He has a huge turban and has casually thrown a scarf over his shoulder. His neighbor carries on his head a crate, made of palm strips, full of *baladi* Arabic bread, on which he has added, in a perilous balancing act, another crate made of palm strips with another load of bread. His small goatee may well be copied from that of rich Saudi princes who are excellent tourists for Egypt.

The modest cart, neither painted nor decorated, offers to the passersby *tirmis* (Lupini fava) soaked in water and salted. The paper cones for the fava are prepared in advance with old newspapers. The *ollah* (terracotta water-jug) is there to quench the thirst of the clients.

An elegant city-dweller well covered with a fashionable veil with trendy colors holds firmly to her bag. She is followed by her maid carrying her daughter on the shoulder, while her brother saunters in front of them in an unusually calm Cairo street.

Once Upon a Time...in Egypt

41

Samir M. Zoghby

13. Don't Tell Me How To Carve the Meat!

Owner of the butcher shop, *el-Hagg 'ali Bunduk,* the butcher is very busy cutting up his meat on a huge wooden block for his clients. Behind him, the many carcasses are hanging from metal solid hooks and naked electric bulbs without shades give a crude light. The big door of the freezer occupies a section of the wall covered with tiles easy to clean with a good stream of water.

The cat, guardian of the place, stares at the conservative clients bundled in their veils.

Once Upon a Time...in Egypt

Samir M. Zoghby

14. The Sweet Smell of Ismaïlia Melons

Market scene. Our client with a modern plain skirt and jacket hides her plumpness with a large scarf, but she has difficulties covering so much territory. She carries a plastic bag. These bags have become the scourge of Egypt, flying all over the place, clinging to trees and polluting the country. The United Nations report that the world uses a trillion bags per year and that 46,000 pieces of plastic float in every square mile of the ocean.

Our client has a multitude of choices...In the back, the fruit vendor offers sugar canes, melons from Ismaïlia—the best in Egypt—as well as tomatoes, and peas, all well stacked on palm tree crates. He has added to his *galabiyyah* a skullcap with bright colors and wears an imposing mustache.

The fishmonger has knotted his handkerchief on his head in the style of Egyptian farmers. He probably offers fresh water fish such as Nile perch. Not far, another fruit vendor does not have as much variety. His oranges are well staked in a crate and his tangerines are in a basket woven with palm tree leaves. The mouse is not happy with the menu!

Once Upon a Time...in Egypt

15. The Young Qena Diogenes

Egyptian countryside scene. Our Diogenes pulls on the tail of the donkey to tease his older brother leading an ewe and its lambs to market. The big brother looks daggers at Junior.

The two young girls are going to the river to wash their heavy cast iron pots. They are wearing pants under a becoming dress with a light veil. They are not covering their faces like their city cousins.

The transport truck is registered in Qena, a town in Upper Egypt, about 39 kilometers north of Luxor. Qena is well known for its pharaonic ruins of Cainepolis as well as its mosque honoring a *sufi* (mystic) from North Africa—Shaykh 'abdel Rahiim—who settled in Qena in the 12th century.

These trucks carry goods but also passengers. The latter climb on the bundles and hang on as well as they can, covering their faces to protect themselves, as much as they can, from the clouds of dust raised by the truck on earthen roads usually made of red laterite. The place near the driver is the first class seat of the service. It is generally occupied by the village notables.

Once Upon a Time...in Egypt

16. Gossiping Al Fresco

In front of a screen made out of braided bamboo, three friends chat while sipping a glass of red tea. One of them is wearing a cashmere scarf with multiple geometric designs and an embroidered *ta?iyyah* (skullcap). He is sitting on a plastic chair, sign of modernity! Facing him, his friend sitting on a carved and painted wooden village chair, draws on his water pipe with ataraxy. The third compadre is wearing a woolen scarf. The brass table is common in the neighborhood cafés and villages. They must be telling each other *nokat* (plural of *noktah*) "jokes" (generally political) for which the Egyptians are know all over the Middle East. These are humorous stories with an acerbic, denigrating put-down and strident finale. They are part of a typical Egyptian humor including the *ishme'nah* (so what?) routine, a sort of verbal duel at a rather shallow level often concentrating on the anatomy of the adversary's mother! In fact the *noktah* has been the only means of resistance, defense and retaliation by Egyptians in a flat country, with a desert where you die of thirst, without forests to hide, a prey to hydraulic despotism[4]—as described by August Wittfogel—where, he who controls the water controls the country. With a ribbon of water snaking its way through the center of the country, how easy it has been for the Pharaohs to

---

4 This was confirmed by Ayman al-Zawahiri, the Egyptian leader of al-Qaeda, who wrote, "The river Nile runs in its narrow valley between two deserts that have no vegetation or water...such a terrain made guerrilla warfare in Egypt impossible." (*The Looming Tower* by Lawrence Wright, New York, Vintage Books, 2007, p. 52).

Once Upon a Time...in Egypt

control Egypt; they were followed by foreigners, from 525 B.C. with the Achaemenids, to 1956 with the British ; and after them by the Egyptian military with Abdel Nasser, Sadat, Mubarrak and now el-Sissi. The brief apparition on the Egyptian political scene of Mohammed Morsi was nothing but an insignificant hiccup.

The vendor has settled her ample derrière on a minuscule wooden stool and is able to maintain an uncertain equilibrium. Stick in hand, she attentively looks after her produces spread on a large straw mat and two baskets to protect them from the prowling animals. The terracotta water-jug is a typically Egyptian model.

The etiquette of the water jug requires that you drink raising it well above your head and let the water flow directly into the throat, with a gurgling noise, without, however, letting neither lips nor teeth touch said jug.

Corporal punishment
mamnuu' el-darb...

"No beating allowed," we used to defiantly tell our teachers beating the bejesus out of us. The law was there—can't remember the number of the decree—but the application was sorely missing and everybody went merrily his own way, the students complaining and fending off the blows as well as they could and the teachers venting their frustrations, their lack of hope, their misery, their desperation on us.

To the point

My maternal grandfather, Nonno Altenburger, was a very direct man. He always said it as he saw it in a very direct and often brutal way. When I was about twelve years old, I decided to build a fishing rod with a reel using a length of bamboo, some strings, and a spool. I was hard at work when he passed by, looked at me toiling, and without a smile or a smirk said simply and plainly, "It won't work," without any concern about today's child psychology and other child-shielding concerns. It was direct and true!

17. And Then, I Told Him...

A group of friends gather near the Nile river to enjoy the waterside breeze and the sunset.

The four compadres sip a strong red tea noisily slurping the hot beverage. One is sitting on the floor leaning against the wall of the terrace railing. He is wearing a modest turban. The other, on a wicker chair, has wrapped his cashmere shawl around his neck and smokes his water pipe following the conversation. He is probably better well off than the others as he wears socks with his Sudanese slippers, often made out of the skin of big cats. The third is bundled in a woolen scarf. He has a turban and leans his invalid leg on his cane. The fourth wears a heavy shawl in camel hair and a well turned turban. He is sitting on a wooden chair made by the village carpenter, who has also built the low table in palm tree wood.

A distance away behind the group, another friend is squatting on the floor. His status in the group is undoubtedly somewhat less important. The boy is pulling a small car made out of a light wood, often palm tree. He is keeping an eye on the puppy who, follows, intrigued, the walking "beast."

Once Upon a Time...in Egypt

18. Old Man and His Donkey

A hot domino game. Two friends are focusing on an old game resting on a wooden tablet. Two others follow the game with great interest. A fourth seems vaguely interested, while the last one is plunged in his mail, probably from his children studying in Cairo or any of the other university towns.

Seating on the curb—recently fixed by the municipality—the vendor praises her fruits arranged on a crate "made in China" while her client well covered by her shawl is looking at her with suspicion. The old villager donning a skullcap well covered by a turban has well secured his straw basket on his donkey. They have known each other for such a long time that the stick and the rope are mere accessories... The stubborn donkey obeys only his master's voice. The old man, warm in his shawl, is half asleep. His companion knows the way...like a Cypriot donkey. Years ago, when visiting my uncle Henri Altenburger who lived in Limassol, Cyprus, I had heard that Cypriot donkeys were well known for being covered with scabs and for recognizing, without ever erring, the way back to the farm.

Once Upon a Time...in Egypt

19. The Ornithologist in His Milieu

His bundle on his shoulder and wearing a derisive smile, the amateur ornithologist finds himself in his universe. He appreciates a beautiful bird cage. The owner, less of a dreamer, interrupts his haggling with a client to praise the merits of the cage to the ornithologist. The young one looks with envy at all these cages thinking that the day will come soon when he will buy himself a large one.

The bearded one is probably an *Ikhwangi*[5] (member of the Association of Muslim Brothers). He is accompanied by his mother, his wife, his daughter and his last-born—a boy *wal hamdu lillah*[6] (Praise be to God). He looks at the cages that have attracted his daughter's attention. The women are all well bundled up including the little girl who hides her thick braid under an embroidered veil. The old man has no beards but a small toothbrush mustache. He has donned an elegant silk *galabiyyah* and has thrown on his shoulder, in a negligent and elegant way, his heavy *'abaayah* (a Bedouin cape made of camel hair) that falls to his midriff.

The other couple is modern but conservative, given the heavy coat with multiple buttons, worn by the wife, that goes to her ankles, as well as the veil twice-wrapped around her head. Her husband is western dressed with a crewcut that seems rather military.

What could the two tomcats tell each other surrounded by bipeds?

---

5   Ikhwangi was a common term, when I was living in Ismaïlia, for the members of the Muslim Brothers Association. It comes from Ikhwan meaning "brothers" to which is added the "gi" of appartenance or affiliation.
One also says:
simsargi - broker
'arbagi - coachman
sofragi - waiter
bohyagi - shoe-shine boy
ahwagi - coffeshop manager
makwagi - presser
afyungi - Hashish afficionando
6   Al-hamdu lillah - Thanks be to God, *Deo gratias*.

Once Upon a Time...in Egypt

Samir M. Zoghby

20. The Village Shisha Is Still the Best!

The cousin of the merchant in Chapter 9 has also a bushy beard. He has a turban and has wrapped a cashmere scarf around his neck to protect him from the morning cold. He smokes a village water-pipe made out of a coconut or a terracotta bowl and a bamboo or carved wood tube. The chair, a copy of the one he is sitting on, is covered with a rich fabric. We are very far from the village chairs coarsely cut out of palm tree wood by the village carpenter. The cousin's shop is well stocked and his shelves are full. The back wall is covered with heavy printed, embroidered, and bazin fabrics that offer the buyer a wide variety of choices. The bazin is a damask cloth where many patterns are woven in the weft. A long and laborious process will make the cloth stiff with a characteristic rustle. The bazin boubous, ample garments for men and women, coming from Mali, are known all over West Africa for their excellent quality. Some Austrian companies, such as Vorarlberg, also produce the valuable and much appreciated bazin cloth.

    Less important than the cousin are two young vendors. One is sitting on a wooden chair with a straw seat, and the other is squatting before a quite ugly plastic low table with two glasses of hot red tea. The stall of the two partners is an ingenious device on wheels which allows them to park it in the store of their elder for a modest fee. The stall offers a variety of shirts: there is one for every taste. One of the partners keeps a vigilant eye on the youngster hiding behind the stall, which is not a good omen! The cat quietly follows the conversation of the two partners without bothering too much about the mouse that reigns in the shop.

Once Upon a Time...in Egypt

21. Morning Trades

Morning finds various workers at their tasks. Pushing his heavy tricycle loaded with hot and crispy *baladi* bread, the baker hurries up to deliver his goods to his clients. The young passerby took advantage of the situation and bought a bread which he munches on with delight. The baker has an *ikhwangi* beard and is modestly dressed with pants and a T-shirt; the heat of the oven is certainly the reason why he is scantily dressed. As for his son helping him push the tricycle, he is wearing modern style Bermuda shorts that are the rage of the day.

The jovial fellow pushing his bicycle on which hang several aluminum milk jars dons a turban precariously balanced on his skull. He wears a cotton *galabiyyah* and a vest adorned with multiple buttons. He goes from door to door selling his milk. His robust bicycle is made in China.

When I was a kid, many tens of years ago, I often visited my paternal grandmother in Cairo. This citadel of the family was Lebanese and very proud to be a member of the *Yared* family and to belong — said she—to the prominent "Seven families" of Beirut. Every morning about six o'clock, the calm of the neighborhood of Faggalah was upset by the passage of a herd of goats noisily led by the chief shepherd and his sidekicks. The herd—about fifteen goats—was the mobile milk reserve. They stopped by most houses, and people gave them a container. A goat was quickly cornered and the shepherd milked it. The milk was nicely lukewarm and delicious. The custom must have been abolished by a municipal edict produced by a bored paper pusher prohibiting goats to circulate in the streets of Cairo which deprived the neighborhood of a good morning milk.

It is still too early for the mustachioed peanuts vendor to find clients at this early morning hour. But as he is walking, he plans to slowly push his four-wheel cart towards a *midaan* (square) not very far from the ministerial buildings where some civil servants would go strolling. The well decorated cart shows the ex-voto *Ya rabb* (O God). In addition to peanuts, the cart includes a number of glasses and water-jugs to quench the thirst of the customers. His mended clothes and his sandals, probably cut in old tires in Ho Chi Minh fashion, suggest that his commerce is not too flourishing.

Once Upon a Time...in Egypt

Samir M. Zoghby

22. Camel Transaction

Morning transaction. Two traders conclude the sale of a camel. They are dressed in *galabiyyahs* and their heads are covered with turbans cleverly wrapped. The camel has been bathed, groomed, dolled up and wearing its best attires. A number of woolen pompoms adorn its bridle and its saddle is embroidered with woolen geometric designs in shimmering colors and the two leather pommels have been waxed and shined.

The introduction of the camel in the Middle East and Africa has radically changed inter-regional and trans-Saharan trade. The camel is a secure and inexpensive means of transporting bulky and heavy merchandise over long distances. The camel can travel for days without eating or drinking and his round flat feet allow it to easily walk on sandy expanses. In Somalia, where is located the largest concentration of camels, the latter is called by at least 46 names. In Arabic, there are names for all types of camels, such as the *Mehari*—a dromedary for racing and long distances. There are names depending on the number of times a camel drinks (once, twice or many times a day); names for the characteristic features of the animal and names according to its color. The history of Arab literature reports poems written by Bedouins praising their beloved camel.

In the camp, it must be early in the morning as the youngster in the back is stretching and scratching his back while eying the fritter of his youngest sister. His other sister, wears a long dress with a flower pattern and has a small necklace of multicolor glass jewelry; her head is covered with a light scarf matching her dress.

Once Upon a Time...in Egypt

His older sister is busy washing clothes in a pewter basin. She wears a veil that covers head and mouth. She is very proud of her typically Bedouin necklace and heavy wrought silver bracelets. His aunt is also dressed Bedouin style with multicolored beads on the forehead and a large necklace covering the front of her dress. Her heavy veil covers amply her head. The mother is busy with the last born, a boy. He is the undisputed master of the encampment! His mother also wears a Bedouin dress with a veil covering her head and pearls hanging from her forehead. A triangular veil covers her mouth; it is generally covered with silver coins linked to the forehead pearls by a silver cylinder. She too is proud of her heavy silver bracelets. We thus see that the dress of Bedouin women is very different from that of female city dwellers and farmers.

Ancestry and scholarships

When I was working with the US Agency for International Development in Yemen, I was responsible for the Scholarship Program. To avoid pressure that I knew was coming, I had bought a large (10x6 feet) batik portrait of then President Ali Abdallah Saleh that I hung in my office, and I acquired a copy of the Yemeni equivalent of the Libyan Green Book. I was ready. It soon did not fail to happen. One officer came to "talk." He said that he was happy that a Zoghby, whose ancestors came from Yemen (which is true), was in charge of scholarships. With a big grin (that reminded me of the Arab poem that says: if you see the canines of the lion shining, don't think that the lion is smiling) and caressing his holster that held an impressive Tokarev, he leaned towards me and said, "I want a scholarship to the US for my son." I grinned back, showed him the portrait of the president, and opened the little book at the four principles of the Revolution and pointed at the one stating, "All Yemenis must have equal opportunities." Our guest got the message five over five.

Student demonstration in Cairo
Yahyal Wafd we law fiih\a rafd...

Long live the Wafd (the first and major political party in Egypt, created in 1918) even if it means being kicked out of school. That was the rallying cry of students marching in demonstrations against the government.

Samir M. Zoghby

23. Village Cunning

Often to entertain themselves in the villages, elders organize stick jousts. These jousts are called *tahtiib* coming from the word *hatab* (wood). The bludgeon is called *nabbuut*. The game is also called *al-fann al-naziih* (the virtuous art). The young men of the village defy each other to fight and often after joust enactments, similar to the Kata exercises in Judo, fight "for real" which sometimes ends up with the interventions of the judges' acolytes to separate the jousters. The champion of these fights is the village hero and he will challenge the champion of the next village. I have vague memories that at the age of six or seven I have attended such jousts in the *'izbah* (farm) of a friend of my father in the Nile Delta, where we often went for weekends.

The joust is organized on the village square, surrounded by palm trees, not far from the mosque where a group of spectators incite the fighters to surpass themselves. A trio of judges insure that the rules of the art are rigorously applied and, in case of a dispute, decide who the winner is. The two fighters watch each other with great attention to take advantage of the least hesitation that would allow him to bring down his bludgeon on the bludgeon of his adversary. The inhabitant of the village dons a modest cotton *galabiyyah*. One of the judges has thrown his valuable shawl over his shoulder in a haphazard way while his colleague is covered with a large woolen shawl. Two others sport turbans that cover their skullcaps.

Once Upon a Time...in Egypt

24. The Redskins in Aswan

Not everybody can work with marble. One must be strong enough to handle heavy slabs and precise enough to avoid wasting the precious stone.

These three workers labor in a quarry, probably near Luxor, not far from the Nile as did their pharaonic ancestors who carved by hand the marble for the sumptuous villas of the Egyptian elite many centuries ago. But these workers are more lucky as they have at their disposal modern saws to cut the marble with precision and speed. One wears a *kufiyyah* and a European vest. His cigarette never leaves his lips! The other one dons a denim suit that was probably given to him by a Greek foreman who had a short-term contract with the company. The third one is wearing a Redskins T-shirt supporting the Washington home team. It was given to him by a diplomat from the American Embassy in Cairo who accompanied a congressional delegation (codel) studying the marble industry in Egypt and had taken advantage to make the classical tourist circuit.

Two children are bemused by the modern machines. One of them is black, he could be the twice-removed grandchild of a slave brought back a century ago by Egyptian slave traders from the Sudan which is not very far.

Once Upon a Time...in Egypt

Samir M. Zoghby

25. Lost in His Newspaper

Baab al-Hadiid (the Iron Gate) is the main railway station in Cairo. It was built in 1856 By Saïd pacha, the vice-roy of Egypt. A fire destroyed the station in 1882—maybe at the instigation of the British who occupied Egypt that same year? Nobody knows! The station was rebuilt (1891-1893) by a British architect. In 1928, a large statue called Egypt's awakening made by Mahmoud Mokhtar, the famous Egyptian sculptor who studied at the Paris Ecole des Beaux Arts in 1911, was erected in the square as a symbol of Egypt's nascent nationalism and a testimony to its long history. In 1955, after the revolution of Colonel Gamal Abdel Nasser, the statue was replaced by a colossal, 36 feet high and weighing 83 tons, statue of Ramses II (who ruled from 1279 to 1213 BC). The revolution changed many street names including Shaari' Malikah Nazli (Queen Nazli Street), where lived my maternal aunt, that leads into Midan Baab al-Hadiid (Baab al-Hadiid Square). Queen Nazli, the spouse of King Fuad and mother of King Farouk, was the granddaughter of Colonel Joseph Anselme Sève, a French officer who served Napoleon at the Battle of Trafalgar. He joined Mohammed Ali, the founder of Modern Egypt, whom he served faithfully. Sève is the founder of the new Egyptian army. The statue of Ramses II was moved in 2006 to the atrium of the new Cairo museum because pollution risked destroying the monument.

In the hubbub and confusion of that station that serves Cairo, a train is entering the station. Two women apparently conservative and well covered look at a young man sitting by his bundles. He dons a turban over a *ta?iyyah* (skullcap) with geometric designs. He seems to contemplate on the palm of his hand his Apollo line and his destiny line that should indicate—according to some

Once Upon a Time...in Egypt

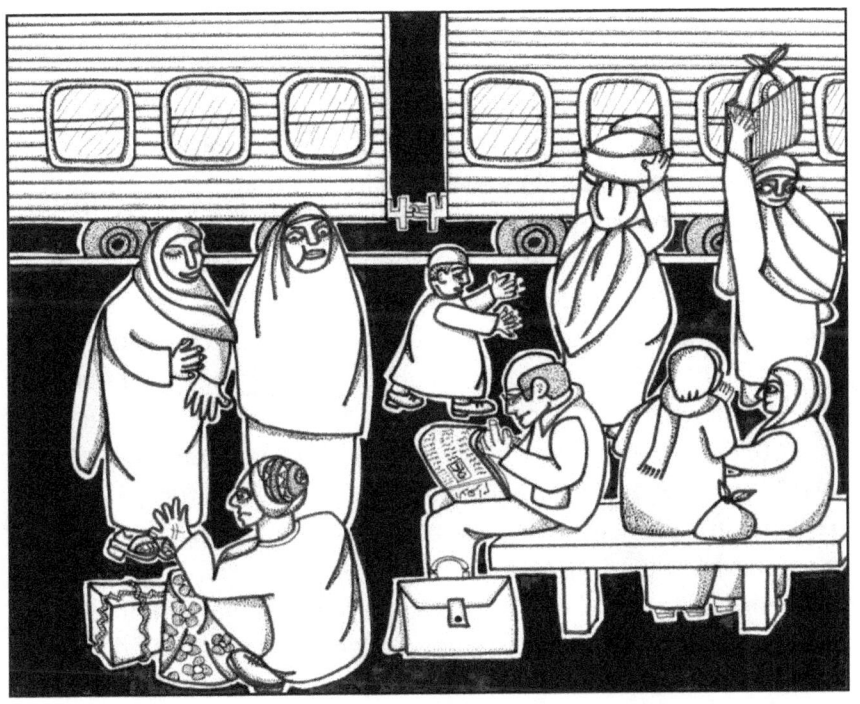

palmists—all the events that took place in his life since his birth!

Sitting on a bench, a bald and myopic intellectual, his leather case at his feet, is oblivious of the world surrounding him and is diligently focusing reading *al-Ahraam* (The Pyramids). This newspaper was created in Alexandria by Salim and Bichara Taqla, two Greek Catholic Lebanese brothers. The paper became a daily in 1881 and its offices were trashed during the revolt of Colonel Orabi in 1882. Was it the British who were already sapping al-Ahram which had published articles by the religious reformers Mohammad Abdo and Gamal al-din al-Afghani? The Orabi revolt ended with the occupation of Egypt by Britain in 1882 and lasted until 1956. With the help of two other Christian Lebanese, Ya'kub Sarruf and Faris al-Nimr, the British are said to have funded the creation, in 1889, of a rival newspaper, al-Muqattam (name of a chain of hills southwest of Cairo) to support the British viewpoint in Egypt. Al-Ahram has gone through many changes and vicissitudes particularly under Abdel Nasser and his advisor and confident Mohammad Hassanein Haikal, who was its editor for many years. Salah Jahin, the famous cartoonist, lyricist, poet, and actor who gave dialectical poetry its just place in Egyptian literature, has also worked for a long time at al-Ahram. He was a great admirer of Gamal Abdel Nasser to the point that he was called the "poet of the revolution."

Today, the al-Ahram is still accused of representing editorially the viewpoint of the government in spite of the denials of its various officials and editors.

Sitting not very far on the bench, but neither too close to the intellectual, two women with a small bundle are chatting while waiting for their train. The other two women loaded with baskets on their heads are hurrying up to find an empty wagon while worrying that their kid following them, not without difficulty, does not get lost in the crowd. They have finally found their wagon, and the kid did not get lost. As for the intellectual, on the other hand, he missed his train as he was immersed in his newspaper!

Bedouin fortune-teller
Adrab el-raml wa shuuf el-wada'...

"I look into sand and consult sea shells" was the call of the Bedouin woman passing under the window of my grandmother in Ismaïlia. Nonna would threaten to give me to the wild woman if I did not behave. I behaved.

Divine diva
Ya suuma...

... a cry of ecstasy during the long drawn-out musical events of Umm Kulthum, the eternal and unsurpassed queen of Arabic love songs. Her multiple repetitions of stanzas hypnotized her public, peasant and minister as well as known level-headed intellectuals. People gladly spent a month's salary to attend one of her concerts that lasted long hours and to see her tear her diaphanous handkerchief during the long drawn-out vibratos.

The government train
Law faatak el-miiri, itmarmat fi turaabo

If you missed the government train, roll in its dust. If you failed to get a cushy government job, linger at the periphery. You may get some crumbs.

73

Samir M. Zoghby

26. Ford and Chevrolet Trucks on Dusty Roads

A peasant and his heavy bundle try to hail a truck in a village, not far from the town of Assiut in Upper Egypt (the road sign shows: Assiut—35 Kilometers). Assiut, the old Greco-Roman Lycopolis, is situated halfway between Cairo and Luxor. The city is located in a very fertile plain, and it is the starting point for caravan trails leading to the oases west of the country. It was also the beginning of a trans-Saharan trade route towards West Africa in the Middle Ages. This city of 400,000 inhabitants of the seat of a Governorate.

According to its license plate, the Ford truck is registered in the Governorate of Assiut. The passenger, completely covered by a veil except for a slit for her eyes is sitting quite stiff near the driver, who is looking as serious and respectful as he can. The overloaded Chevrolet with bursting parcels and crates full of fruits and vegetables is going full speed as the (reckless?) driver has blind faith in the protection provided by his *ex-voto* painted on the rear of his truck: *Tawakkaltu 'ala Allah* (I put my trust in God)[7]. He too has a license plate from the Governorate of Assiut. The donkey is not a mechanic although he is trying to stick his head under the hood of the stalled car. The two youngsters offer to help the distressed driver out, for a modest sum, and to pull his vehicle with the donkey to the next garage. The ultimate humiliation! The private car is also registered in Assiut. The main street of the village is paved...the *'omdah* (village mayor) has good contacts in Assiut!

---

7 Tawakkaltu 'ala *Allah*—I put my trust in God, God is my support.

Once Upon a Time...in Egypt

27. The Legacy of Hassan al-Banna

Very young in Ismaïlia, I remember the credo of the Muslim Brothers plastered on all the walls of the town: *al-Islaam diinun wa dawlah, qiyaadah wa 'ibaadah, sayfun wa qalam* (Islam is a religion and a state, leadership and worship, a sword and a pen). I also remember, during World War II, the same credo co-existing with a red hammer and sickle on the great white wall of a hotel belonging, presumably, to a sympathizer of the communist regime.

The Muslim Brothers movement was created in Ismaïlia in 1928 by Hassan al-Banna, a primary school teacher, who was revolted by the impact of Western influence on the inhabitants of the town and by the debauchery of the soldiers of His Very British Majesty in the bars of the town. At this time, Ismaïlia was the Headquarters of the British army, situated at *Moascar* (the Camp), as well as the Headquarters of the Suez Canal Company. The town, in fact, belonged to the Egyptians only in name. The British army and the Company ruled and ran the Suez Canal Zone, particularly after the beginning of hostilities in North Africa and the successes in 1941 of the Afrika Korps (DAK). The Muslim Brothers are the source and inspiration for the great majority of fundamentalist movements in the world. In Egypt they were fought by King Farouk, who ordered the murder of Hassan al-Banna, by his Iron Guard, to avenge the murder of the Prime Minister Mahmud al-Nukrashi Pasha by the Muslim Brothers after the Prime Minister abolished the association (the story is much more intertwined and complicated than that!). They were also fought by Presidents

Once Upon a Time...in Egypt

Samir M. Zoghby

Abdel Nasser, Sadat, Mubarrak and el-Sissi. Always after a brief honeymoon between the Muslim Brothers and the various regimes.

    A kid is having a hard time following his mother loaded with a large bundle tied with a heavy rope. Her head is covered with an ample fringed shawl that covers her loins. The trio of well-veiled women pass by rapidly in front of a man who shows the faint beginnings of a smile. He wears a heavy *galabiyyah* and a shawl on the shoulder. Two of the women chastely lower their head while looking down, the youngest one looks at them to see how she should react. Trotting on his burro, the man has wrapped his turban around his neck like a Mauritanian desert *hawli* (long turban that covers the head and the face of men). He and his "passenger," as well as his burro, are concerned about the dog approaching in a menacing manner showing its fangs. The stick will probably calm the hound if it wants to avoid a beating

Cairo and the Champs-Elysées
Masr omm el-Dunya...

"Egypt is the mother of the world." A politician friend was visiting Paris. He was strolling along the Champs-Elysées with my father, who reminded him, in jest, of that proverb. The friend looked at him, then looked at the famous vast avenue and answered, "Not even her cousin!"

Guerrilla warfare in the Suez Canal

In 1952, during the guerilla activities against the British, the latter had occupied Ismaïlia and set up road blocks all over the city. There was one right by our house. One day, we hear gunfire. Our servant Nur, a Nubian giant almost 7 feet tall and weighing 300lbs, was ironing in a room facing the street. He suddenly, after a loud shot, came to my mother, mumbling: el-rosaasah , el-rosaasah ya sett (the bullet Madam, the bullet) and fainted in the arms of my mother, a rather small person. He had come too close to the window and the bullet, which we later found in the room, missed him by a few inches. We kidded him for a long time.

28. Pink Nightgown and Somber Darks

On the threshold of her wrought iron door decorated with vivid and garish colors, stands a young woman with a scarf on her head and lightly clothed with a nightgown that shapes her bountiful form. She has a smirk on her face while looking at a group of women dressed in a most conservative fashion pass by. Two among them don long dresses, a veil on the head and a *niqaab* (veil covering half the face). One of them is wearing gloves that show only the wrist. The little girl is also drastically dressed. She is looking at her companions who, although wearing dresses all the way to the ground and a broach with the name of Allah, have not covered their faces.

Near the door is a *ziir* (terracotta large jar) with water to quench the thirst of passersby. A goblet is set on a wooden stool. The *sabiil* (public water fountain) is the gift of a pious and wealthy man. It is the equivalent of the Paris Wallace fountains as mentioned in Chapter 11.

Once Upon a Time...in Egypt

29. Hurry Up...We Must Catch the Train

A group of women are hurrying towards...who knows what! Maybe to catch a bus or even the same train at Bab el-Hadid. They are all differently dressed. The one on the left dons a heavy dress that goes to the ankles. A veil covers her head, a *niqaab* hides her face and she is wearing gloves. The others are also dressed modestly with veils covering their heads. The student on the right is only wearing a light veil on her head with a small modern knapsack. The jeans are ample and do not outline her silhouette.

Once Upon a Time...in Egypt

Samir M. Zoghby

30. Free Parking

An old district in Cairo with an old door under a medieval arch and a wall covered with dilapidated mosaic. The municipality has installed a parking lot in the neighborhood. We find the large and spacious American car side by side with two camels harnessed with saddles embroidered with woolen threads of various colors. They are surveying the world passing by below with their usual and natural disdain. The owner has tethered them to a fire hydrant as the leash is too short to do otherwise. The burro, held by his master, is not at ease to find himself so close to the camels, who are known to have a mean temper and would not hesitate to send a long stream of greenish spittle on them or even bite him. His master seems to share his opinion! The cart is well decorated with triangles cut in the wood and painted with bright colors.

    A woman of a certain age with overflowing charms but well wrapped, carries an *offah* (straw basket) on her head from which emerges a duck inspecting its ambient universe.

31. Jerusalem Blue Glass Artist

Ali Abdel Razzak has studied at the Applied Arts Section of the Fine Arts Faculty as is indicated on his diploma hanging on the wall of his master glazier shop. He is busy shaping a Jerusalem blue glass bottle. His counter is cluttered with his very specialized tools and a large gas canister that feeds his gas torch. In a showcase against the wall, and in another in the front of the shop, he displays the products of his skilled hands. This includes perfume bottles of all colors, glass teapots, carafes and bottles of all kinds and shapes. He deals with fire and glass with an expert hand repeating the ancient gestures of his ancestors—probably in the same neighborhood—to create the same delicate and precious articles without, however, the butane gas canister!

The hall of the entrance to the shop is covered with a tribal carpet from the Western Desert oases or even maybe from the Fezzan, a Libyan region North of Chad. His showcase is surrounded by a turned wooden handrail made by the cabinetmakers settled in the next neighborhood. A youngster looks with admiration at the expert handle the glass and the torch. A possible client with an imposing turban and wrapped in a large cashmere shawl hesitates before putting in an order. The woman wearing a wrapping embroidered scarf is waiting for her husband before putting in her order. She is intimidated by the artisan with a *zibiibah* (literally, a dry raisin), named for a growth on the forehead caused by hitting the floor during the five required daily prayer. It is also an ostentatious sign of piety. President Sadat is said to have been very proud of his *zibiibah*.

Once Upon a Time...in Egypt

32. Noon Prayer

In a grove, far from the noise and the traffic, three men pray in an area prepared as a worship space. The low wall surrounding the area has been nicely decorated. A clean mat covers the ground. In a corner is the teapot for the required ablutions before prayer. The rounding in the wall indicates the *mihraab* (generally an arcature and two columns indicating the *iblah* or direction of Mecca) towards which all good Muslim must turn to pray.

Once Upon a Time...in Egypt

Samir M. Zoghby

33. You Squeeze Them, You Buy Them!

A street swarming with activity as are most streets in Cairo. A barber is lathering up soap with a shaving brush to service a client while briefing him on all the latestst rumors, gossips and fibs in the neighborhood. The chair of the client is the last model recuperated from a junkyard, a reject from the downtown modern barbershops. A large mirror covers a span of the wall and an abundance of perfumes and creams await the clients. His neighbor, the dressmaker is at his sewing machine—a Singer naturally—repairing a tear in a garment brought by an old man telling him his woes. The dressmaker must be prosperous as the well tied-up packages, waiting for the clients on the shelf behind him, indicate the important volume of his business.

In front of the shops, a vegetable vendor is shouting at a customer handling somewhat roughly the delicate produce in his cart. It shows the same ex-voto: *tawakkaltu 'ala Allah* (I put my trust in God) as the big truck of Assiut. This ex-voto is very common in Egypt. The woman with a bundle on her head is covered with a big shawl; she discreetly is having a laugh listening to the exchange between the vendor and his potential client. In a corner a modest vendor, sitting on a mat before his meager arrangement of vegetables, hopes to take advantage of the altercation to sell his produce. The cat examines the tray made out of palm tree leaves without great interest.

Once Upon a Time...in Egypt

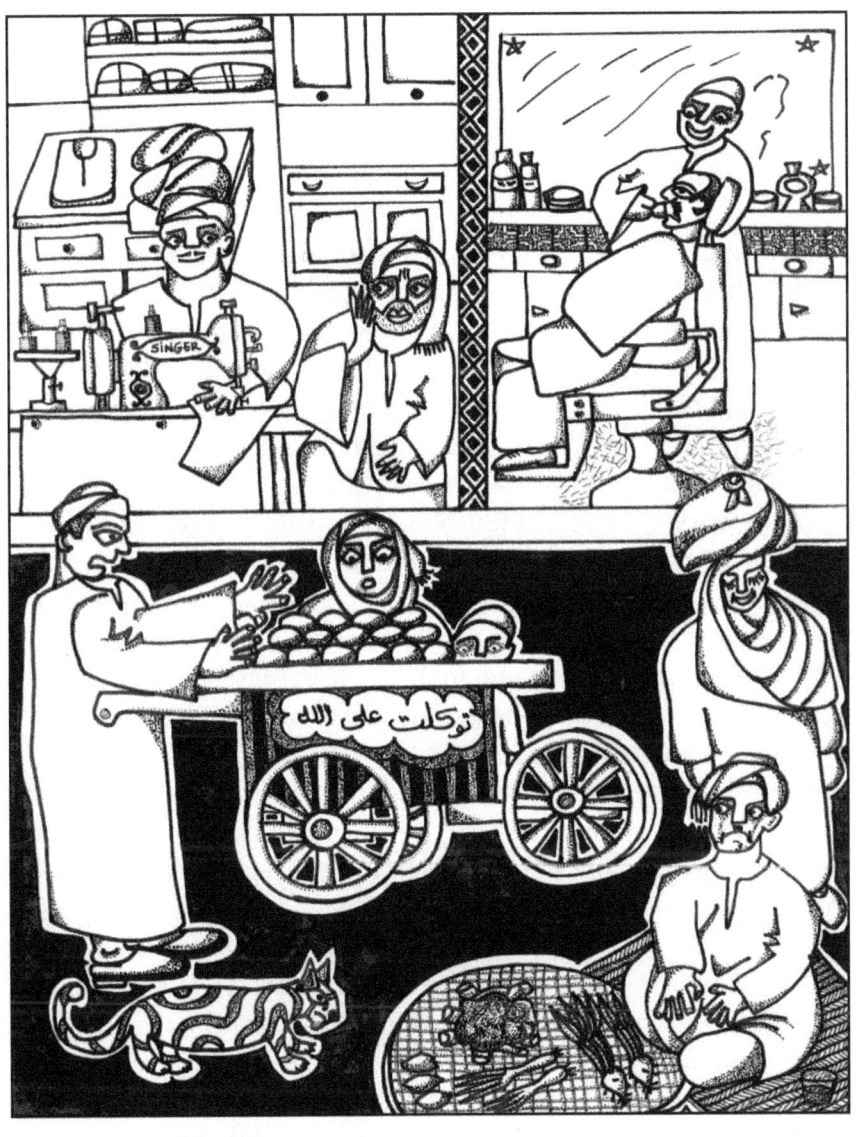

Samir M. Zoghby

34. Working Alabaster in 113 F. Temperature

A workshop of artisans working alabaster in a district of Luxor. The workers have stretched a large piece of printed cloth to protect them from the implacable sun and heat of Luxor. Temperature can reach 113 in the shade in August, if shade could be found! On a shelf behind the men, the traditional *ollah* (water jug) is competing with the omnipresent Coke bottle. The boss, with a top quality *galabiyyah* and a rich scarf around his neck, examines a pot his workers have just finished. He too wears a toothbrush mustache. Another worker, sitting on the ground, hammer in hand, displays a goatee Saudi-fashion and a turban that falls back on his shoulder. He dons a vest with multiple buttons. His comrade has rolled up his sleeves to be more at ease. He skillfully shapes a pot out of a chunk of alabaster. He has a modern haircut and a pencil mustache. He may be thinking that at the end of the day, after a good shower and dressed in a pair of jeans and a low buttoned flowery Hawaiian shirt, he could stroll in the city streets not far from the major hotels. If he is lucky, he could meet one of those European or American tourists, a woman between two ages, or rather of a certain age, looking for a one-night stand of pleasure without tomorrows in the arms of a solid fellow who will give her his "best" in exchange for a generous *baksheesh* (tip). One has heard say that sometimes, only sometimes, the young man would make a sacrifice and "service" the husband as a bonus.

The low table exhibits the products of the workshop for the tourists who stroll in the city. There is a pharaoh's bust, and various pots and vases in alabaster. The young Black, the sad result of slavery that was rampant in Egypt from the 7th to the 19th centuries, attempts to tame the fat tomcat.

Once Upon a Time...in Egypt

35. The Welcome and the Threat

The relentless efforts made by Egypt to combat terrorism, as indicated in Chapter 2, are considerable. Major undertakings and important means have been mobilized to counter this scourge that saps the efforts of Egypt to securely and safely develop international tourism. Tourism is a source of enormous revenues for the Egyptian Government who has invested a lot in its tourist infrastructures in order to attract tourists and convince them to come and spend their vacations in Egypt.

The "Welcome to Luxor" sign could seem anachronistic above the mobile shield behind which a soldier from "Central Security," as indicated by the sign above the shield, is taking shelter. He is wearing a military helmet, is armed with a Kalashnikov and scrutinizes the terrain with much attention and seriousness. Nearby, an Isuzu with a sign reading "Police" is full of soldiers just in case of an emergency. In front of the roadblocks, a military, together with two policemen in mufti, look at a beautiful specimen of a German shepherd specially trained to detect explosive and assist against eventual terrorist attacks.

The policy of the Government seems to give satisfactory results in spite of some attacks which are very difficult to counter in the murky, shadowy and unpredictable universe of terrorism.

Once Upon a Time...in Egypt

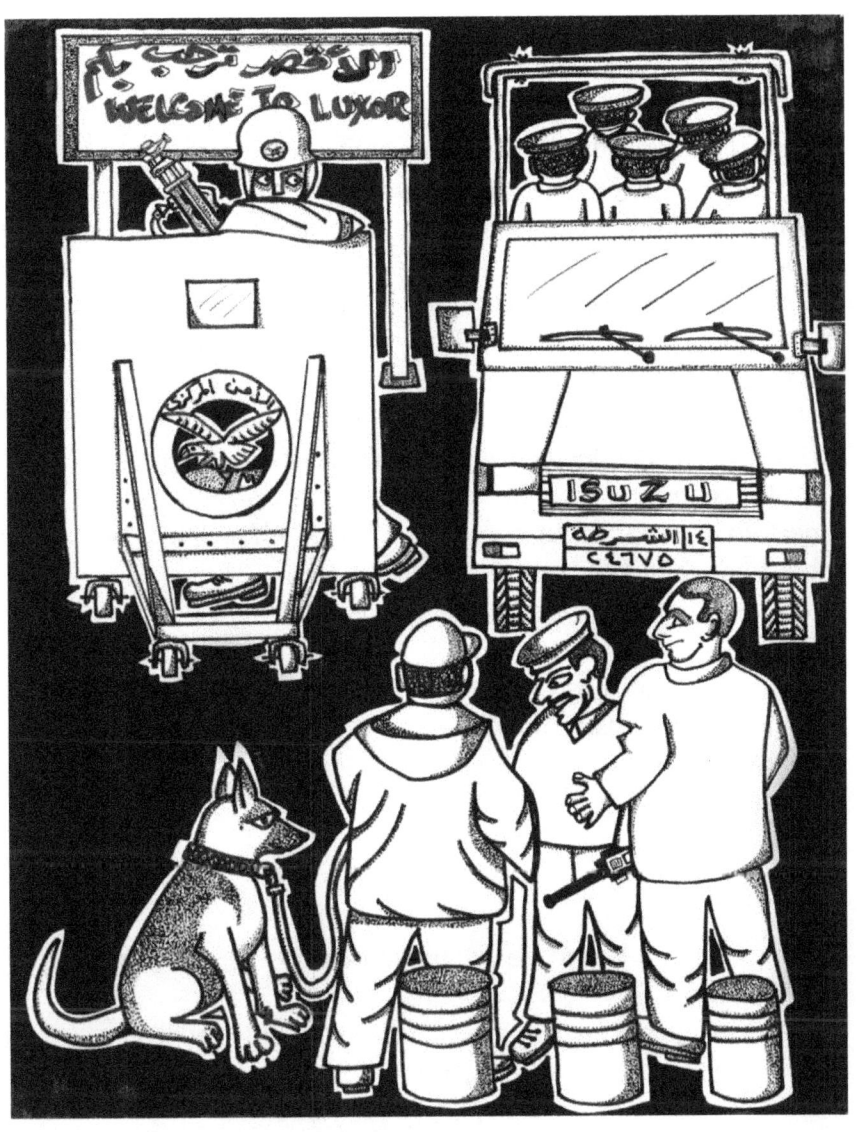

36. Dervishes for Tourists

The whirling dervish dance is a show that always attracts tourists. The former belong to the *Mevlevi* sufi Muslim order founded in Konya in the Ottoman Empire in the 13th century by Sultan Veled, the son of Jalal al-Din al-Rumi (1207-1273), the great Persian mystic to perpetuate the teachings of his father. Sufism, or Muslim mysticism, is akin to all internal spiritual disciplines. The follower identifies himself with the All-Mighty as it was well put by Mansur al-Hallaj (858-922) when he said: *Anal Haqq* (I am the Truth) and for which he was killed by the Caliph al-Muqtadar (895- 922). Louis Massignon, the eminent Islamic scholar, was the great expert on al-Hallaj, to whom he devoted his whole life to help us know, understand and appreciate him.

Al-Rumi wrote:

I saw my Lord with the eyes of the heart.
I asked "Who are You?"
He answered "You."

He also said:

Knock
and He will open the door.
Vanish
and He will make you shine like the sun.
Fall
and He will raise you to Heavens.
Become nothing
and He will make you everything.

which is not very far from what Lao-Tzu said in the 6th century BC in his *Tao Te Ching*:

Once Upon a Time...in Egypt

Samir M. Zoghby

> Those who know do not talk
> Those who talk do not know
>
> Keep your mouth closed.
> Guard your senses.
> Temper your sharpness.
> Simplify your problems.
> Mask your brightness.
> Be at one with the dust of the earth.
> This is primal union.
>
> He who has achieved this state
> Is unconcerned with friends and enemies,
> With good and harm, with honor and disgrace.
> This therefore is the highest state of man.

During a whirling dervish session, *sama'* (harkening), the orchestra is generally made up of musicians playing the *taar* (a large frame drum), the *darabokkah* (chalice or goblet drum), the *mizmaar* (sort of traditional clarinet or horn) and finger cymbals. A venerable dervish directs the dancers. At the sound of *ayin* (traditional musical compositions) the dancers start their gyrations very slowly at an increasing rhythm where they extend their arms, with the palm of the right hand raised to the sky in order to receive the grace of Allah, and the left hand pointing to the earth to spread the grace of Allah until they reach ecstasy and exhaustion. The tourism company that has organized the pseudo-session for the tourists has meticulously prepared the scenario. But the young dancer disturbed it when, before going on stage and in an excess of zeal, he grabbed two frame drums. This was out of script, because the hands must remain free to join heavens and earth in the dancer's gyrations. Children have strolled on the stage, including a young Tyrolean wearing a *lederhosen*.

The General at mass

Once a year, the Suez Canal Company organized a "consular Mass" for the governing bodies of the city and its notables, Christian, Muslim, and Jew. As my father, a cadre of the company, worked on a daily basis with the officials of the city and knew them well, he was asked to receive them on the threshold of the church and lead them to their assigned places. The Egyptian general, stocky and with a paunch, arrived with his second-in-command, who was rather tall and lanky. My father received them at the door and led them to the first row, indicating their respective places, and returned to the door. But unfortunately, there was a kneeling bench in front of the chair on which the general and his assistant sat down facing the public, with their chins resting on their knees. Hearing some commotion and a few laughs, my father hurried back and whispered, "On the chair...on the chair!" The general, good-natured, answered him, "and how the hell do you want me to know where to sit?"

God took the healthy one

I had a younger brother who was a very healthy child and died at the age of three. My maternal grandmother told me many years later that my mother was crying at the funerals muttering, "God, you took from me the one in good health and left me with the sickly one." Yet, the sickly one became a rotund and funny 86-year old senior.

Samir M. Zoghby

37. Conviviality Among Drying Sheets

The buildings of Cairo often have terraces where people wash and dry their linen. The terraces sometimes have one or two rooms rented to people of modest means. A whole social activity has therefore developed on the terraces to form a separate microcosm of its own.

Clothes are drying on a wash line. Seating on a bench, a young university student has come to visit his grandmother. She puts her hand with tenderness on his knee and he wraps his arm around her with filial affection. The two friends of the grandmother, one dressed traditionally and one in Western style, maybe a Greek lady, a longtime friend when everything was fine, listen with great interest to the stories and anecdotes of the young man. As for him, he hopes never to live *'as-sath* (on the terrace) but rather climb the social ladder.

On a large rug spread on the floor, a family takes a simple meal. The father wearing a *galabiyyah* is accompanied by his daughter who has not covered her head; by a son who has just returned from school as he is still in his school uniform, and another son with a patched *galabiyyah*. The grandmother, covered by her veils, is urging the young one to eat. On the rug are various dishes and a green onion. There is also the traditional *ollah* (terracotta water jug) to quench their thirst after the meal. Near the communal faucet a young mother, she too covered with a big veil, washes her son. There are often cats on the terrace. They hunt mice and other vermin.

Once Upon a Time...in Egypt

38. To Hit or Not To Hit?

A great celebration at the village. A marriage, a circumcision, or a visit by a notable. When people organize such festivities, also on the occasion of funerals, they install in the street large panels of patchwork with traditional patterns drawn from Muslim architecture. They are hung up on long wooden posts, to form a large covered hall where chairs are set up for the guests around the central space. This makes it possible to receive a lot of people.

Here, for the occasion the village has organized a *tahtiib* competition. The fighters are accompanied by a trio of musicians to stimulate and encourage them. There is the *taar* (frame drum) this one carried on the shoulder with a halter, the mizmaar (traditional horn) and a drum that you beat with slender drumsticks.

The jousters begin with a series of traditional movements simulating a fight before beginning the joust. Then, the real fight begins and they turn in circle to create the propitious occasion to lower their *nabbuut* (bludgeon) with force on the adversary's *nabbuut* to the shouts of joy of the audience.

Samir M. Zoghby

39. The New Generation Doesn't Known How...

Three streets after that of the barber are two shops. One traditional with an old fashioned cloth press operator. He irons with a heavy metal iron that he manipulates with his foot, the clothes spread on a low table. To avoid getting a foot burnt, the iron is partly covered with a length of wood. To humidify the clothes to be pressed, the man takes a large quantity of water in his mouth from a water jug or a metal can well opened to avoid cutting himself, and spits it out with force on the garment to humidify it! The operator, advanced in age, is traditionally dressed and sports a large turban and a greying beard. Today the younger generation prefers to use charcoal cast irons, or even electric ones that are much easier to handle. The other shop is more modern. It belongs to a young entrepreneur who sells pressed juices. There are mangoes, bananas, and oranges. His shop front is decorated with ceramics. He has invested in modern and brand new equipment: a fruit juicer and a stainless steel sink. The two clients are wearing *galabiyyahs*. One of them has a turban over a skullcap. They have a whole range of choices.

Just across the street passes a pickup truck driven by a Nubian who probably had to abandon his native village in Nubia inundated due to the construction of the Aswan Dam and the creation of Lake Nasser. He has accepted three passengers on the top of his van for a small fee. One seems in a better mood than his companion, but he risks losing his slippers. The goat has, undoubtedly, the best place and is the more comfortable of the four!

Once Upon a Time...in Egypt

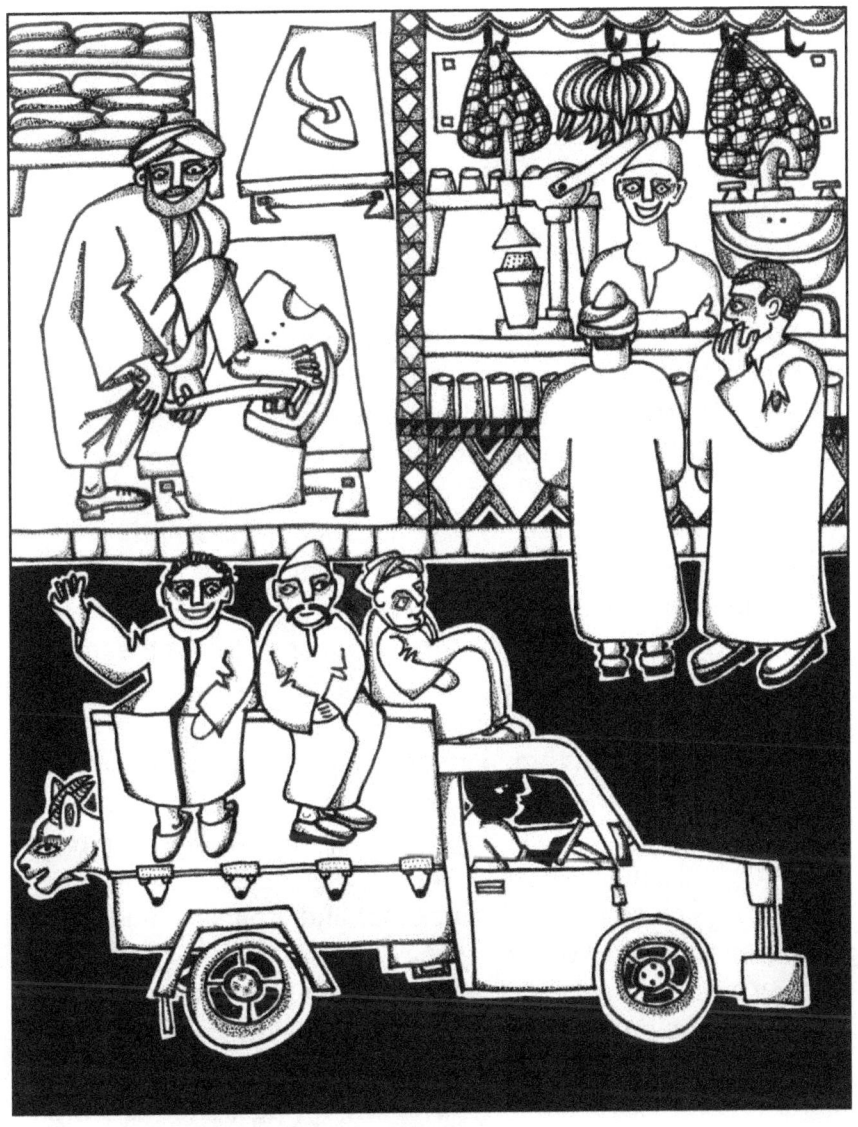

Samir M. Zoghby

40. Darting Looks and Plumpness

Not far from the cloth press operator, in a street as busy as the other one, there are two stalls. One is occupied by a fishmonger donning a Western vest and a large well wrapped turban. The door of his cold storage room is not very far in case he needs to restock his display of fish. He comes from Port-Saïd in the Canal Zone. We know it because his sign reads: *samak al-Bolt* (Bolt Fish,) the local name of this city situated at the confluence of the Suez Canal and the Mediterranean Sea. He has large fish such as carps and mullets as well as an enamel bowl full of small sea-breams to fry whole. He looks with much interest at a client haggling with his neighbor. This one, a young fellow with a modern mustache and very neat *galabiyyah* is proud of his stall. There is *zayt alzaytuun* (olive oil) from Tunisia; *deglet nuur (*light date) and queen of dates from the oasis of Togla in the region of Biskra in Algeria; tea from Sri Lanka; and a multitude of fruits and vegetables. Some are set on crates made from palm branches and others on modern wooden crates. The woman holding on firmly to her bag and wearing a veil on the head gesticulates with force as she is not happy with the price asked by the young mustachioed man.

    A peanut and *libb abyad and libb eswed* (squash and sunflowers seeds) vendor pushes his brightly decorated cart with geometric designs and displaying on its side the inscription *Tasaali al-Gowharah (*Passatempo the Jewel). Paper cones prepared in advance with old newspapers are kept in a hazardous slant on the cart. He also has a plate full of guavas. One has the impression that the youngster in T-shirt looks at the mountain of peanuts with

great envy. By his side a venerable sheikh sporting a full grown white beard, a turban and a beautiful silk scarf looks with mistrust at his plump and well-endowed neighbor, in spite of the great efforts she deploys to hide her charms under heavy layers of cloth and veils. Is she imploring the All Mighty to spare her the acerbic and severe comments of the man of God?

Pulling on his reins, an *'arbagi* (coachman), urges his horse on as he is late delivering a huge crate and an enormous well-tied bundle that he got from the wholesaler. He is obviously proud of the decoration of his cart that has real tires and imposing shock-absorbers in order not to shake his merchandise on roads that are not well paved and full of potholes. The horse is in good health with a nice round belly.

Ignoramus

My father was so much at ease with the three languages (Arabic, English, and French) and knew their grammar rules so perfectly well that he considered me an ignoramus, as I did not know all the mysteries and intricate arcane rules of these languages. One day, exasperated by my abysmal ignorance of these rules, he looked at me for a long time and in a severe tone said, "Listen to me, study your three grammars; otherwise you'll end up as a dragoman taking tourists around the Pyramids."

Dilemma

I swam before I walked. Every year, the city of Ismaïlia organized a swimming race across Lake Timsah. It was roughly five kilometers (about 3 miles) long. I trained assiduously and when the day came, I was ready. We plunged and we paced ourselves. My strategy was to race fast, then, after distancing the competition, to slow down and catch my breath. The winner was always Mohammad Bakhit, a cadet at the Military Academy, who was in top shape. We all accepted that he was the best. He was up front, I was second, and I was trailed by a third competitor. Suddenly, one guy behind me called for help. What to do? Stop and help, or continue? Tough dilemma. I finally decided to race and help the fellow and saw my competitor pass by on his way to second place. But something looked fishy. Before the race, I had seen the two huddling and talking sotto voce. Suddenly it dawned on me that they had a deal to delay me. Cursing the guy, I raced as fast as I could but arrived only third!

41. Enough is Enough!

The Egyptian "Movement for Change" also known as *kifaayah* (Enough) was created in 2004. It was a popular movement triggered by the inertia of Egyptian political life; by the stagnation and inefficiency of political parties and by the dichotomy Secular-Islamist that blocked dialogue between the various component of society. The immediate reason was the rejection by the Egyptian people of a fifth mandate for President Hosni Mubarak who has been in power since 1981, and his efforts to insure the succession of his son to the presidency. The movement attempted to unify the people in a vast political force to face up to the moment's crisis. It was an innovation that did not last for multiple and complex reasons.

During a demonstration organized by *Kifaayah,* one can see an old bearded man from the Muslim Brotherhood, carrying a huge sign reading *Kifaayah*, joining a woman, but she is veiled; youngsters in tank pants and a family man with his son on his shoulders. The security forces, *al-Amn al-Markazi* (Central Security) are well organized to face up to the demonstration. A wall of shields held by well-equipped soldiers protect a warrant officer and a lieutenant in uniform as well as two sergeants also wearing protective helmets. The organizer of the demonstration, wearing a shirt with the motto on his back displays an *Ikhwangi* (member of the Muslim Brothers) style beard. The dog is adding his barking to the cacophony of the moment.

Once Upon a Time...in Egypt

42. The Meal the Pharaohs Ate

An old neighborhood of Cairo that has known better days. It was around 1867 that Cairo, under the reign of Khedive Ismaïl, grandson of Mohammad Ali, founder of modern Egypt, was modernized. A number of 'Haussmannian' buildings,[8] often planned by Ernst Behler, a Swiss architect, were built between the city and the banks of the Nile. This infatuation for this type of buildings is the result of the visit by Khedive Ismaïl to the Paris Universal Exhibition where he discovered the "triumphant Hausmannism" of the French capital. Cairo henceforth included two juxtaposed cities; the old city that had undertaken no innovations and the new city organized Western style which made Jacques Bergue, the eminent orientalist, say: "Cairo is like a cracked vase and it will not be possible for its two parts to be welded together again." After the revolution of 1952, these buildings were abandoned and left to decay. Today, only a few rare ones in good shape are left in Cairo. A very interesting book on the subject of the old symbols of a sumptuous past era is: *Dust: Egypt Forgotten Architecture* by Xenia Nikolskaya published in 2012.

The sign on the corner shop announces *al-'ishaawi—fool we falaafel* (al-'ishaawi fool and falaafel). One also says *fool Mudammis* (simmered fava). Fava are considered the national dish

---

8   Hausmannian buildings. The renovation of Paris (1853-1870) was a vast public works program commissioned by Emperor Napoleon III under the supervision of Georges-Eugène Haussmann, the prefect of the Seine District. New buildings in a typical ornate style were built overlooking the new large boulevards, wide avenues, parks and squares.

Once Upon a Time...in Egypt

in Egypt. They are very much appreciated by all Egyptians, rich or poor, intellectuals or peasants, Muslim or Copts. The aficionado agree that fava must slowly simmer the whole night before being enjoyed the next morning. The bourgeois and the rich often, but not always, serve them for breakfast with hard boiled eggs, onions, lemon juice, a pinch of cumin and much olive oil. It is also the main meal of the peasant who eat them with an onion that he crushes with his fist to soften it. On the other hand, *falaafe*l are also very much appreciated in Egypt and the whole Middle East. It consists of a garbanzo or fava paste, rolled into balls and fried in very hot oil. The crunchy balls are often eaten as a sandwich in a *baladi* bread with pickles, and a *Tihiinah* (sesame paste) sauce. *Falaafel* are sometimes called *ta 'miyyah* in Egypt, but not in Alexandria! Why? *Allahu A'lam* "God knows best."[9]

Al-'ishaawi himself has put the shoulder to the wheel and serves an early client a portion of fava. The two *idrah* (brass cauldrons) contain the precious favas and keep them hot with the help of a butane gas heater. In the street, a vendor of potatoes has stopped his cart adorned with painted motifs. The client well bundled in her heavy veil manipulates somewhat too much the merchandise as is shown by the reaction of the vendor not far from reaching a point of irritation. A young woman and her son look with curiosity at a young farmer leading his sheep to the corner butcher. The woman is dressed Western style, but her long dress is reaching the ground and her veil is doubly knotted around her head. Her son dons a pretty suit and wears a pair of fancy sunglasses. The ubiquitous cat inspects his territory.

---

9   *Allahu A'lam* God knows best or only God knows.

Who taught you how to drive?
elli 'allemak el-sewaa?ah zalamak...

"He who taught you how to drive did you a disservice," one should calmly tell the driver who rammed his old jalopy into your new Maserati.

Speech writer

A story my father told us: Trilingual, my father was totally at ease in Arabic, French, and English. One day the company organized a meeting of the four authorities in Ismaïlia, namely the Chief-Engineer of the Suez Canal Company, the Governor of the City, the general of the Egyptian armed forces, and the general commanding the armed forces of her very British Majesty. Each was supposed to make a speech. And it happened that my father found himself applauding the four speeches of the officials, speeches that he had penned.

Royalty and red cars

When I heard that Ford said, "Any customer can have a car painted any color that he wants so long as it is black," it reminded me that throughout my youth in Egypt, the only red cars I saw were the royal Mercedes, Bentleys, and Packards as well as the fire engines.

Samir M. Zoghby

43. Life is Suffering

Three old men sitting on a bench and leaning against an old wall listen to a trio of musicians, or troubadours, sing a saga of the good old days. The eldest with a heavy *galabiyyah* has thrown a shawl over his shoulders to protect him from the morning chill. He has an imposing turban and seems to be in pretty bad shape as indicated by his helping cane. The second friend is in better health but seems to be in a pretty bad mood. As for the third buddy, he is lost in a distant dream following the tribulations of the heroes of the bard's saga. Two of the musicians are playing a *rabaabah* (two-string viola or fiddle}. The first on the left dons a ceremonial kaftan and a scarf that falls to his midriff. The second musician strikes with vigor his *taar* (frame drum). The third strumming his *rabaabah* intones an epic song about his tribe, relating their adventures and exploits during their migrations from Yemen or other parts of the Arabian Peninsula towards more hospitable lands, such as Egypt, where they sometimes settled and became farmers cultivating the vast Nile Delta.

The Nile, it is said, is the longest river in the world snaking its way through Africa for 4,259 miles. The White Nile, starting in Rwanda and Burundi, and the Blue Nile, starting near Lake Tana in Ethiopia, merge in Khartoum in the Sudan to form a single river. The water resources of the Nile are shared by eleven African countries. This sharing of water is a highly political affair and many experts predict that the next war in Africa will be a war over water. Already, Egypt and Ethiopia are in litigation over the Ethiopian Grand Renaissance Dam that the latter is building on the Blue Nile near its border with Sudan.

The village children listen with fascination to the troubadour relate their history. The young Black one is Nubian and his parents were forced to leave their native village when it was flooded by Lake Nasser.

Once Upon a Time...in Egypt

Samir M. Zoghby

44. Veterans of the Dark Days

The village coffeehouse with its rustic tables and chairs with straw seats made by the local carpenter. The low wall hides the river where grow palm trees and water lilies. There is always a light breeze coming from the Nile.

Four old friends steadfastly discuss politics after the events in Cairo which led to the eviction of Mohammad Morsi and the return of the military to power. They share the same ideology and are great supporters of the Muslim Brothers. They come from Ismaïlia and are first-hour companions of Hassan al-Banna, founder of the movement he created in this city in 1928. They have gone through hard and sorrowful moments of persecution during their lives and have been incarcerated in the "House of Corrections," reserved for political prisoners of the infamous *Abu Za'bal* Prison. This section was the breeding ground of the movement's militants. Sayyid Kutb, who is considered the theoretician of the Muslim Brothers, was jailed there. He was executed by Abdel Nasser in 1966. That triggered a process where, after a brief honeymoon and period of collaboration, the Brothers became the sworn enemies of Egyptian military regimes who pursued their members with relentlessness and hatred. The feeling, one must admit, is reciprocal!

The first friend on the left, has a bushy beard partly covered by an elegant and finely woven Cashmere shawl. His turban is well rounded. He carries a cane to help him walk. His leg wound, received during the harsh interrogation sessions at Abu Za'bal, is still hurting him. His friend wears a sleeveless leather jacket on a

Once Upon a Time...in Egypt

galabiyyah. His blooming beard, the *zibiibah,* mark of his religious fervor, on his forehead, and the newspaper of the Muslim Brothers that he is holding clearly indicate who he is. The third friend is another veteran of the Dark period in the history of the movement. He too carries proudly a *zibiibah*. This asperity appears on the forehead of pious Muslims as they bang their forehead against the floor during their five daily prayers. It is a sign of piety and rigor. He is wearing a turban and carries over his *galabiyyah* a beautiful embroidered scarf. The fourth friend dons a kaftan open in the front showing his multi-button vest. His beard is smaller than those of his friends. On the other hand, he has wrapped his head in a *kufiyyah* over which he has a heavy woolen shawl.

    The fall of Morsi was a great shock for this group of veterans. It did not astonish them the least...It is an old story...the pattern repeats itself with the regularity of a Swiss clock...Collaboration with the government in power followed by the persecution of the movement by the latter. Nothing new since the time of their assassinated leader Hassan al-Banna in 1949.

Great expectations
'ashshimtini bil hala?...kharamt wedni...

"You let me hope that you'll buy me earrings, I pierced my lobes." When people hint that they'll give you something or do something for you and then they renege, you blurt this proverb.

Human coil
Ya zambalek...

O [wonderful] coil! A roar of admiration addressing belly dancers such as Tahia Carioca, a famous belly dancer in the late 40s and early 50s, during their gyrations and contortions.

Ping pong at the Muslim Brothers' club

When I was 15 years old, I liked to play ping pong. Once in a while I used to go to the Club of the Muslim Brothers in Ismaïlia to play with Muslim friends. Once a hard and pure Muslim brother saw me playing at the club. He was not happy and asked why a non-Muslim was playing ping pong at the club. My friends answered that it was OK as my father was a friend of the Supreme Leader. I guess I am one of the rare Christians to have played ping pong at a Muslim Brothers club.

Samir M. Zoghby

45. The Chanting of the Word of God

A young man enters a building adjacent to the mosque where *Tagwiid* (Chanting of the Koran) is taught. The importance of the Arabic language in Islam is primordial. The reason is that God, who has dictated the Koran to the Prophet Mohammad through the intermediary Angel Gabriel, spoke in Arabic. The All Mighty said in the *Surah* of Joseph (XII:2): *Inna anzalnaah\u qur?aanan 'Arabiyyan la'allakum Ta'qiluna* (We have sent it down as an Arab reading so that you may reason).[10] The first person who made the call to prayer, the *Azaan* at the time of the Prophet is Bilal Ibn al-Habashi, an Ethiopian ex-slave and companion of the Prophet. The latter has preferred this method to call the community to prayer rather than the use of bells, like the Christians; or the use of the horn such as the *Shofar* of the Jews.

Tagwiid is the way to chant the Koran as prescribed by the Angel Gabriel who taught it to the Prophet. In the *Surah* (Bundled Up, LXXIII), it is said: *Wa rattili l-qur'aana tartiilan* (and chant the Koran distinctly). The *Hadiith* (the tradition, or sayings and communications of the Prophet) recorded and verified by the six canonical compilations of the tradition, differentiates between what God said in the Koran and what the Prophet said during his life. One *Hadith* reports that the Prophet said: "In fact, Allah desires that the Koran be chanted as it has been received." Various "Reading Schools" were created during the 7th and 8th centuries of our era, each with its particularities such as the schools of

---

10 Translation by T.B. Irving (al-Hajj Ta'lim 'Ali)

Once Upon a Time...in Egypt

Medinah, Mecca, Basrah, Damascus and Kufa. Very precise and defined rules were developed during the 9th century by Abu Bakr Ibn Mujahid (died in 936) that systematized the rules for an appropriate chanting of the Holy Book.

The youngsters who attend the koranic schools spend years memorizing the Koran. Their mastery of this art is put to a hard test by *Tagwiid* competitions. The slightest mistake, infraction of grammar, or change in the tone or rhythm of the chanting is severely sanctioned. I remember, thirty years ago, attending such a competition at the Grand Mosque of N'Djamena in Chad. The building of the mosque was funded by Saudi Arabia, seeding already the Wahhaabi grain in the Chadian soil. A fifteen-year old youngster stood in front of an audience of seasoned Chadian Muslims. He looked quite worried and tense. He started the chanting with much assurance, but in the middle of a sentence he made a pronunciation or inflection mistake, The furious audience, exploded in a tsunami of complaints and shouting correcting the poor youngster who was completely destabilized. Nevertheless, he was able to complete his chanting with the encouragement of his teacher. This showed the zero tolerance of most Muslims for mistakes in the psalmody and the visceral reaction of the audience to a failure, no matter how small, in the chanting of the Book of Allah.

Bribery
Ya salaam, shuufu shoghl el-khawagaat...

"Look how wondrous is the work of the Khawagaat (the foreigners)," said the head of an equipment selection committee, who had been bribed by my paternal uncle, when presented with defective material, and he approved the deal before any member of the committee had time to react and object.

BBC and the 1956 War

One day in October 1956, during my junior year at the American University of Beirut, my advisor, Professor George E. Kirk, a British national who had a colorful life during WWII, called me into his office. He told me that a group of examiners from the BBC were recruiting for the Arabic programs of that august institution and asked whether I was interested in interviewing for the job. I agreed, telling him that I was finishing school the following year and a secure job with the BBC was a great opportunity. The following day, a Friday if I remember correctly, I had a very British interview that was successful, according to Kirk, and the two fellows told him that they were interested in recruiting me. But luck was not on my side that day, as on Monday, October 29, the Tripartite Aggression, or the Yom Kippur War, or the Ramadan War was launched. The two examiners disappeared and I never worked at the BBC.

www.ingramcontent.com/pod-product-compliance
Lightning Source LLC
Chambersburg PA
CBHW051346040426
42453CB00007B/431